ISLAND

ahsahta press

The New Series

number 7

ISLAND

POEMS BY CHARLES O. HARTMAN

ahsahta press

Boise State University • Boise • Idaho • 2004

Ahsahta Press, Boise State University

Boise, Idaho 83725

http://ahsahtapress.boisestate.edu

Printed in the United States of America

Cover art: Found map of Aigina, courtesy of the author.

Author photograph by Wendy Battin.

Book and cover design by Janet Holmes.

First printing October 2004

ISBN 0-916272-80-X

Library of Congress Cataloging-in-Publication Data

Hartman, Charles O., 1949-
 Island : poems / Charles O. Hartman.
     p. cm. -- (The new series ; no. 7)
 ISBN 0-916272-80-X (pbk. : alk. paper)
 I. Title. II. Series: New series (Ahsahta Press) ; no. 7.

PS3558.A7116I84 2004
811'.54--dc22

                                    2004009172

for Wendy

Contents

TAMBOURINE

Now: 3
Echoes return   7
X   8
Blood struts lordlier   11
And I can compass stepping out   14
A humdinger   16
Attention   19
Villagers abruptly   20
All these paths   23
Following   24
Whatever X builds   27
I reckon I keep going   28
Afternoon going for climbing   30
Surely   31
Panegyric   34

MORNING NOON & NIGHT

The Thousands   41
Orrery   42
Nothing Waiting   43
Tureen   44
Gift   45
Fascination   46
In Shreds   47
The Woman with Terrible Eyes   48
Hollows   49
Dummy   50
Sorites   51
Doves   52
The Octopus   53
The Disappearance   54
In the Hands of the Breezes   55
Not One   56

The Unknown   41
That Land   42
Lottery   43
In the Afternoon   44
Behind the Village   45
All Ways   46
A Labor   47
Accidents   48
A Paperweight   49
Crowd Control   50
The Apotheosis   51
Planning   52
A Vocation   53
Plot   54
Visible End   55
On the Beach   56

The Stones   57
The Mission   58
Egg Salad   59
Ticket   60
The Collector   61
Clear   62
Piece by Piece   63
The Cloth Bag   64
The Mountain in the Middle   65
Outdoor Theater   66
New Mown   67
Stepwise   68
Philippic and/orJeremiad   69
Libation   70
Syzygy   71
The Responsibility   72
The Door   73
The Sands   74
Misplaced   75

Unaccountable   57
Crocodile   58
Colossus   59
South   60
On the Rack   61
Corner   62
Along the Coast   63
Line of Duty   64
Offering   65
History   66
Faculties   67
A Certain Hour   68
The Message   69
Levels   70
Order in Disorder   71
Stay   72
Tide Pool   73
Ready   74
Glimpse   75

EIGHT GREEK LYRICS

Το Τηλεφώνημα   78
Νεκρή φύση   80
Ονειροκρίτης   82
Ο Ράφτης ο μεθυσμένος   84
Κατάσταση   86
Το Τραγούδι της ακρίδας   88
Στη Παλιά θέση   92
Νησί   94

The Phone Call   79
Still Life   81
Dreambook   83
The Drunken Tailor   85
Situation   87
The Song of the Grasshopper   89
In the Old Place   93
Island   95

WHERE AM I   97

NOTES   105

Tambourine

*Also, he made a molten sea of ten cubits from
brim to brim, round in compass… and a line
of thirty cubits did compass it round about.*
—2 CHRONICLES 4:2

Now:

I walk a coast brilliant as dragon glass
        for water flinging splinters chaotic alongside
                and in the distance long orders of island
                        spun for the occasion out of morning
                        corporeal light

As mythical violence sets a bloodline running
        a cooler intention now
                austerely furnishes the horizon broad O

Light examines me

Isometric leaning wind
        beatifies this mind
                grown credulous as air

Vagrant entirely
        I borrow time

Giving in
        finesses giving up

Electing something devouring
        finesses giving up
                superbly

Now this universe at large has lost an I
     I
          locates

Seeing invents
     otherwise anywhere
          is a same nonplace

Nonsense errant
     makes a bid to submerge it all

Tumult sieges each boulder

Assiduous its breakers
     maul each island

Buggerall stops still

Three quarters of an age
     I devoted to sloth and worry
          nearabout dead

Whenever I do halfwise
     that dreadful I O U
          closely held
               grows

No rockdove says I

No pelican

A cumbrance
      for voyagers
            lined in a V

Being human makes traveling
      harder with some reason
            if it compounds with becoming
                  pleasures worth
                        just traveling for

The variable I
      rehearses values
            that like to approach constant X

Character happens while selves attend other urgencies
      and the form that unseen X is
            intuited from vividly drawn dreams
                  mind projects on the odd daytime seascape
                        barely noticed produces
                              the I Steady Stand
                                    or phantom I am

X
      saturates

Meanwhile I walk miles graced
      with circling gulls
            storks lofted
                  garnering
                        of the very island

The very searocks exhale X

Most truth lies
        but in strict rhythm lies
            accuracy in a way
                now arbitrary
                    now direct

Measure is action

So this metrician
        X says I am
            squares the spheres
                we hear
                    every footfall
                        centers

—————————— 0 ——————————

Inland for a sight
    climb passages
        reciting a history
            each mountain bespeaks a piece of

Orogenies do

Narrative yearns
    to continue
        as geography
            is never done

Expansion a century a digit
    has charms even the wholly frantic
        educated gradually to
            might apprehend

Not simply

—————— 0 ——————

X
    I say
        can

Rocks may

Water says
    counting enchants it

Each figure trains waves to a new hypnotic ease I have
    copied painfully
        while I confirmed
            when I seize X
                X eludes

Cuchulain
    hews the sea

Waves
    trouble at nothing

Yet taking scant thought
    water
        toothless
            gnaws senseless a shoreline
                rawly new

Possessed of a brainpan
        facing X
            I blinked
                yes
                    grasping a mischance for it
                        facing X I forbore
                            mymisself and I

Known X
    I imagined
        would lose vitality

Suppose that this heresy be now finally abandoned
        supposing dinner is frankly more startling after having
            starved for years a hopeless abnegant quite tightly
                woven in weblets of self dominion espousing
                    a by no stretch universal law
                        relieved
                            I remember now

I a patchwork from wayonback
    I an epiphenom emergent
        for the moment
                compact for the moment am
                    hard work

Suited labor charms
    fervor
        past due

Peripaty counts

As a day convolves
      this clockwise pace around the perimeter
            turns on an edgy craving for mastery
                  I recognize

Roaming

As a century convolves
      peramble counts

Songlines
      tune
            the travels

So rhythms thicken

Timed for walkabout by a skysign
      I measure myself by milestone for a roadway
            sandal leather takes on the waywiser
                  with nearly nothing left unproven I discover
                  this merely walking making living
                        seriously
                              fine

Mused
      I say so

———————— 0 - 0 ————————

BLOOD STRUTS LORDLIER
        I do believe
                a body given to taking
                        joy where bidden

Fortunes in delight pervade anyplace sense awakens
        example
                a guy with an octopus
                        turns seawall
                                through thorough thwacking
                                        tender

Elsewhere
        a rooster too dimwit for morning I suppose
                blithely hollers at a blue heaven overhead
                        lust loud

Splendoes

I am an eary gathering
        quiet
                and loud too

A boat passes
        laden with wayfarers
                steam sounding forth his initial O

Oomph

Echoing pulsation of an echoing pulsation
        voices vitulate broadcast
                on every timeworn frequency
                        to get their word in

A helpfully undefined limit
    namely I
        f of X
            am listening

So a quodlibet
    begins

Creation
    pushes back

The next cape I navigate
    a coast brilliant etcetera
        a new manner of arranging reality
            repeats that nothing
                masters a day

Impatient
    prodigity rounds

Wryly
    a fraction escapes

Mindful of X
    I set down whichever dimension
        whichever magnitude
            whichever direction suggests the vectors
                of veritably pilgrim progress

Most theolatry bullshits about X

Since doctrinal middens are a pitfall
        out of courtesy
                X eludes

Hindsight
        traces out
                a rambling
                        bound
                                territory round

It maps
        this value beginning with
                three point one four
                        wooing expansion

Fabulous day

An ardent toil of
        prowl it is
                too

Plenties of hours
        and for each word
                twenty trancing steps

The heart is speech
        a perimeter
                and I
                        a rational diameter
                                I address X

O

AND I CAN COMPASS STEPPING OUT
        sideways without being an untoward outaline
            faring paths findable
                between wants
                    and has to

Wherever
        and whenever I need to

Behind a hillock
        a further hillock arises
                series
                        extending I feel
                            endless and

Not right naturally
        interior is bound and thus
                reachable

Just as Odyssean cursive trips trace some Aegean bestiary
        showing how a π might designate
                areas easily as limiting curves for divagate argument
                        so the lines any venture overland between hills describes
                            all meander about a
                                peninsula minus isthmus
                                    finally spelling
                                        a babbling drawl tending
                                            Ithacan
                                                homeward

After all
        if I signify
                I do it before thinking

Chance
    choose a way

—————————— 0 ——————————

A HUMDINGER
    of another stairway
        notated mutely
            begins C D E
                ascending
                    agile intervals

Logarithm of a scalar
    step
        up

A monotonic goatbell
    somewhere off
        confirms

Harmonial
    scads of birds
        entitle me

I

Beyond where this hillside climb declines
    giving way to gentler geodesic tangents
        beyond where indulging the sloped
            a craze
                has had setbacks
                    I plodding or lightly
                        gravitate toward
                            desiring to fly

How

I delectate
      going to

And going too

A peculiar piece of highblown rustic rhetoric ricochets aimlessly about various
      heights the better to be heard overabove headwinds that a sun stiffens
            hazarding a no less fruitless descent to a muddled echoing depth
                  to validate the most fuckwit theophany I ken
                        a dance I dance
                              quite elegant with practice
                              quite regular
                                    to walk to talk
                                          being
                                                what I heard

Memory
      producing music
            reabsorbs music

Fanfares no orchestra belts out
      and I a player
            resonate around a network of earshot
                  focusing every nerve
                        rewarded
                              spirally receptive

Valleys
      sound

Listening minutely for
    instance I saunter
        along this saddle
            all yawning ears
                noting what melodizes the formulary
                    for X
                        economies of scale aside

Stride

Rite

—————————— 0 ——————————

ATTENTION
    is telling
        measure

A needle
    seeking X
        I pay attention

————————— 0 —————————

Villagers abruptly
      this rambling
            populate
                  in kind

I go fumbling
      among palatals and velars
            a barbar

Old women darken
      the benches

Donkeys
      loudly abound

O

They radiate X

A sentence I construct from my halfassed lexic hoard earns gestures toward
      a planetree shielded whitewash cool minute taverna
            inside looking suitable for someone
                  more sore footweary even than foreseen
                        to drink amply and appease clamoring stomach
                              happily with company if mutely
                                    mouthing each forkful
                                          O

Good

Good heavens
      mercy how late things have gotten to

Goodbyes

With speech hooked together
        just
                we build farewells

Ritual exchanges bind everybody
        I am persuaded
                all via a few
                        rococo
                                singing phrases

In timefast
        mouthworn formulas
                naturally
                        I speak an I

With similar grace
        am I spoken to

After speech
        guestgift beside
                amazed

No shit

Seven apricots

The angelist
        a child

A messenger for which
    X I be sworn
        who now reselect
            my lone way

——————————— 0 ———————————

ALL THESE PATHS
    untimely decline
        except this

It goes lilting into cloudless heaven
    like someone who is chosen for gallantry
        a road I gleefully recognize
            as company to esteem

With an oblate afternoon ascending so
    to optimal parabolic climax
        slowing steadily
            as now
                takes hold
                    playing gravitas
                        I follow its camber

———————————— 0 ————————————

Following
    and lost
        I startle at a glance
            what I in a hastiness perceived as wild
                paths resemble alleys
                and I climb

Old

To evacuate coasts
    a ratsnest of murderous pirates
        they built these steep streets

Eleven hundred year anamnesis
    sheathes the impacted walls

Round town helically from plain upthrust
    revolved solid
        churches strewn
            countless as houses elsewhere
                numbering
                    every annual saintsday

Boulevard
    up springs
        as S

Traffic
    thinkably
        crowded aloft

Abandoned now

As centuries press forth
    out of X
        X builds again
            the town
                once
                    realities resorted equally to

To decades quiet lanes
    peoplings retend

Or not
    either bond
        haunting

Either mortar holds fast
    tenacious guarantee
        a T buttjoint coupling normally
            I likewise fit
                just another transient
                    knowing whither bound and
                        where finger plucks the thread
                            stretched lifelong

However long or lopped short
    ever it loves to vibrate urgently
        tensed to pitch
            draws a notation
                a likeness
                    a ghostly shape visible like
                        hollow village
                            in emptiest readiness

Desertion
    revives silence
        resting lightly
            on hearths
                perfected for sleeping

———————— 0 - 0 ————————

Whatever X builds
    time empties

Enough

———————— 0 ————————

I RECKON I KEEP GOING
        on some plenitude I construct
                as a present
                        and as a habitat
                                as a daft diagram
                                        pointed to one south

I find I have lost a carefully ordered
        and quite nicely balanced daily mind recently
                I expect I was giving X a nasty asspain
                        for plans no worse given up I see
                                for mere delight
                                        which finally gets
                                                a complete free pseudopod over things
                                                        excepted only the farthest shore
                                                                as the end of the itinerary

Delight now awakening like a hard sun
        all the body dread made antlike
                recalls Aeacus
                        by Zeus
                                a raised myrmidon cohort
                                        to yield a manifold companion outright
                                                and later render grandsons
                                                        like Achilles
                                                                worth being
                                                                        roused by

Feelingly surprised as a butterfly to be an I
        Aeginant
                body is tickled
                        in every sense

As every inch of nerve
    itches rigorous
        whatever circuit sorely charged
            I inhabit
                persuades

Very temporary
    this engine

I wonder where
    say
        wild horses wander nowadays

This planetary peepshow
    arranges itself
        to mystify me
            and to provide
                sometimes
                    a through composed
                        anthem

Steadily since morning creation puts out
    radiance for radiance
        as someone willingly driven without
            resentful scruple should expect
                whenever X gets mixed into I

——————————— 0 ———————————

climbing the central eminence
ascent for assent

Amazement
rises

Stride shortens

———————— 0 ————————

SURELY
    what is up
        ahead I go
            bound to

Every I
    I imagine
        and construct
            in projected sections
                here
                    directly
                        completes itself

Becoming what I do
    becoming what
        sojourns
            becoming harder to locate
                justifies this lanky rhumba

Step by step
    I
        instructs broken trail
            in mounting
                steep

Up it
    is X

Nobody except X
    a dwelling
        spoken for

Myself looking down this
        no kidding
                thousand cubits of it

And certainly a knowledge that redefines what knows

Once offered
        I is the present I was
                forever promised
                        island centering summit

Whereupon these loaned and lifted eyes con leagues
        I enumerate a horizon
                an infinite perfect line broken without visible damage
                        upon random known islands
                                named islands and recounted islets of this
                                        I see
                                                stranger homeworld

Studious toward every footnote
        jot or tittle
                rapt sight ingathers
                        geography which reflects
                                a day
                                        too
                                                declining

All beckons
        downhill

Ah
     orogasm
          eases
               shoreward

———————— 0 ————————

PANEGYRIC
       unwinding talk
              praise
                     falls overall
                            easily down

Various ordinary graphemes
       enter a no longer terribly hard formal contract
              and forthwith unawares
                     the light of naked gratitude
                            comes dancing

Wavelight reflects
       an order
              obscured
                     as no others do

Order is an urge
       resisted
              sparingly
                     best

History derides an ending
       nothing a landscape does insists remotely
              on ending
                     puzzling what
                            delights in ending

A good measure
       begins
              revolving clockwise

Revolving

An ageold ache

A sun arises and intrigues some mind
        and finally goes under water
                yes

Heart

Number measures it

The most satisfied estate of words to find
        takes a pattern from somewhere
                and assembles windfalls inside
                        since a body has a mind
                                to indemnify likewise

Repeating
        a beginning

Urchin grips
        epochally
                to rocks

Diligence can decline
        to be a wholly worthless burden
                with barely a shrug
                        a small miracle

Attention
        mirabile dictu
                fulfills the peculiar
                        wistful name
                                I

Where attention returns
        mirabile frigging dictu
                generally there amazement equally rewakes
                        as listening
                                engaged
                                        takes over faculties
                                                switched otherwise
                                                        off

A bellow a roaring laugh and posthaste an ecstatic wave speaks lethally
        a ten syllable of itself
                ordained before sunlight yet hitherto always anywhere
                        unheardof with no prudent prelude
                                with a total noisy impudence affirming
                                        a wondrous crass grand certainty
                                                as large as life likes
                                                        shadowing forth
                                                                how hereafter every
                                                                        solitaire will
                                                                                say I

This darkening deposited sealand
        as light as time leaves
                shimmers

Twilight runs under porcelain sealight
    filling in hollows and hiding hill feet
        before spreading along sealanes
            like invading pirate sails
                the nightmen
                    and taking finally the summit
                        so as to finish up neatly

Panegyric amplifies
    a so long
        solong

Minutely

Cries O
    to know
        how anything vanishes
            into the wolflight

Then cries O to know
    when a day begins
        about what precisely
            anybody should be already
                worrying

Looking backwards
    looking forward
        a lucky number
            withholds
                a full and final reckoning
                    seriously teasing
                        closure

Morning Noon & Night

The Thousands

The dictionary lies spread open on the table.
The old spine pulls the pages right,
right back to D, to C… The fan
in the amazing heat serenely oscillating
passes and repasses and shuffles the words toward S,
toward T… The minute cries of the words
fluttering into the air, back and forth, jumbled together
thousands at a time, fill a space
in the middle of the room. Anyone who came in
could take them down.

15.VI.99

The Unknown

In the garden the roses' turn's gone. What's this here?
It's time—he says—to get out the book of flowers again.
And what is that bird singing so violently in the tree,
in the lemon tree? or is it an insect? I wish I had
a book of insects, he says. But wait, before that,
a shape so big it blurred the sun for a moment,
the sun intent on picking out all the flowers
and all their orange, unknown petals and stamens,
is passing right overhead—he says—and now
another the same, but no, different, quite unlike.
And across the road, in the surface of the sea…

15.VI.99

Orrery

By the window, the bucket, in the bucket, the mop
and a foot of gray water. The old man picks up the bucket
and carries it to another corner. Hours trickle down.
The old woman comes in and moves it
closer to the door. In the late afternoon the old man
nudges it with his foot right up to the threshhold,
coddling the mop's handle upright to lean on the jamb.
The water eddies slowly, slows, can barely be seen
moving. With elaborate precision the sun rolls down the sky
to the bottom, and covers itself with sea. Moon comes up,
goes over, the old man and the old woman snore
in turn, like the pistons of an old, old engine.
At midnight the son comes home drunk. No no—
he says—he steps nimbly over the bucket,
then turns and kicks it into the garden.
Earth and the water darken each other, with no one to see it.

15.VI.99

That Land

The stalks of bamboo tick together like claws
all night; the child wakes again and again,
partway, to think about a foreign country. Beside the bed
the parents sit silent, and the grandparents and great-grandparents,
and their parents—rings of chairs. The child
wakes again just enough to think, Everything in that land
wants to eat me; but the child isn't afraid.
The bamboo stays outside the window,
like the almond tree, whose flowers seem to fill the room.

15.VI.99

Nothing Waiting

On the edge of each bud the red bugs are mating,
end to end, mostly motionless. Solitaries
busy themselves on the leaves. Ants run up and down the stems,
some carrying the bodies of other ants.
Beside, in the lane, the lizard leans up and tastes air.
The whole evolves in silence, except for the ground-bass
of bees numbering the flowers. Nothing waiting for anyone.

16.VI.99

Lottery

The blind man works the length of the waterfront
calling out mechanically about the people and their lottery,
and back again, missing the chairlegs and parked motorbikes,
the feet and elbows and coffeecups and curbs. One man buys
five tickets, another three. Along the edge the boats
bob lightly, at random, never quite touching.
Crowding overhead gulls cruise aimlessly and without collision
until a crust drops and draws four to one spot.
The boys on their cycles roll slowly past the tables
trying not to look like looking, seeking
a crossing glance.

16.VI.99

Tureen

The plates, scrubbed, go back to their rack,
the cups to theirs. Then someone hungers, thirsts,
a flurry of activity, then sitting around dirty.
Night spills in and soap comes, and the sponge.
Back in the cupboard, the plates on one side, upright,
cups upside down on the other, the air is stifling,
there is practically nothing to do
but dream of an heroic ideal, a tureen, insurgent,
or an earthquake. As the weeks decay,
a cup flings itself to fragments on the floor;
a plate, cracked, disappears for good;
and every so many months, new, familiar faces
arrive in time for the holidays.

16.VI.99

In the Afternoon

In the afternoon while the town sleeps, a woman
is washing her hair. She rubs soap into it and sings.
As she rubs harder lather rises out whiter and whiter
and spills out her open window into the street,
down through the town, all down to the harbor,
rising higher and higher to the second balconies,
the TV antennas, the weathercocks, the topmasts.
Now the woman begins to rinse her shining hair
and changes to a new song. Slowly the mountains
dissolve like snowdrifts in the sun as the town
begins to waken again for evening.

16.VI.99

Gift

While everything else slows on its way to noon
a cat trots up the road with a lizard in its mouth,
the green tail dangling like a lace. The cat trots smartly,
it knows where it's going, the lizard is a gift
best delivered still twitching. The old woman on the bench
watches jealously. Her hands are eager with needles.
The basket beside her is full of wool and socks.
When she moves her feet, dust rises into the air and stays there.

17.VI.99

Behind the Village

On the mountainside behind the village another village
of beehives, square, white, sepulchral in dry heat.
The sound of the bees simmers among them as the air
shimmers above them. They are under siege, under tribute,
but they know the uses of flowers and all their habits.
Let the people below struggle with newspapers and ignorance,
with ships and marriages and watersports and the milking of sheep
for the yoghurt that yearns so rapturously for honey.

17.VI.99

Fascination

He buys a glass mask; now under the water he can see.
He buys frogfeet to swim to what he sees, and a tube
so he can breathe. After a while he buys a spear
with three barbs, and though he draws the line at a gun with elastics,
now he can impale what he sees. Everything stays away then,
of course, but he is fascinated by his new powers,
he carries his things everywhere in a canvas bag,
and some nights he gets up secretly and in the dark puts it all on
and gazes at his watery reflection in the mirror of the sideboard.
Everyone sleeps, and the soft flopping of his feet through the house
barely disturbs the mice.

17.VI.99

All Ways

Half-light, wolf-light, I have walked to this bench
—he says—ten months a year every evening. The same
bench over the same sea, the same islands on the skyline.
The identical moon, more or less. The star of evening again,
and later the many stars. All ways the same—he says—
except the wayward ways of men, and that except me, my ways remain
unalterable, though not eternal. They say this stone
I tap my cane upon is turning wildly in space, in place
yet also all over! and I believe it. Look at that cloud,
you'd think it was a mountain if you hadn't always seen the mountains.

17.VI.99

In Shreds

Here's that wind again, he says.
It puts feathers and pillowcases on the sea
and sprays the sheets hung on lines over the alley.
It hangs the seagulls still and drives the doves backwards.
The trees would tell you which way it blows
if you were deaf and insensible. It ventilates
the skirts of the widows one way uphill
and the other way down. If I had nails and a hammer
I'd teach it to sit still. (The wind carries
words away in shreds.) But then—he says —
I suppose it would rain.

18.VI.99

A Labor

Very exactly, at dawn the statues resume their attitudes.
This is their hard work. The smoke of day itches them.
Their hands hurt, the ones that have hands.
The hard work of the sea is to move without going anywhere,
move violently both up and down, both back and forth,
which is its secret. The hard work of the birds consists in singing.
The work of stars is to keep track of one another,
work of a lifetime. The work of the mind
is to create, the body's work is to endure it.
The mercy of time is passing, which is its secret.

18.VI.99

The Woman with Terrible Eyes

Walking among the shops, the woman with terrible eyes
casts them casually, carefully down. She does not hurry.
Tell her your secrets—she is like a bank for secrets—
but don't look at her as you speak, in case she might glance up.
The woman with terrible eyes cracks open the heart of the world
like an egg, with one sharp tap of them. Everyone in the streets
talks a little louder when she passes, looks a little more busy.
The air holds its breath around her. Take care, she might
forget, or forget herself, and nothing can prepare you.

18.VI.99

Accidents

In the lot behind the restaurant sits his crumpled car,
just as he said. He lives over the restaurant.
His dog lies on the cool front seat, on her long chain, chin
on the steering wheel, and growls. He went over a cliff
near the next town, tumbled dozens of meters
down the shore. He has a new motorbike
and also a new puppy who chews his shoes, or pees in them,
it wasn't clear, it wouldn't have been clear at all
except that dogs do only so many things to shoes,
only so many things happen to cars near the sea to crumple them,
and people tell only some kinds of stories about their lives.

19.VI.99

Hollows

Moon in the day, never the sun at night.
Water inland, never land long under water
because it isn't called that any more.
In hollows in the rocks, pockets of salt.
Summer coming to term in cicadas' dozing.
Cat in the open window, wrapped, asleep.
In a bed, in the afternoon, a man in a woman.
Fire inside the lantern. Roots in earth.

19.VI.99

A Paperweight

On a shelf in back of the shop is an old paperweight,
a glass globe with an ebony base, in the globe
blue sea-and-air and a blue island, and on the island
a mountain and twelve hills, twenty-seven villages
and five towns, the main harbor intricate with streets
along the waterfront and running back from it
lined with houses and little shops, one of them
with a back shelf holding only a paperweight;
and if you take it outside in the sun and turn it over
the light swirls everywhere in gold flakes.
And this is why—he says—our days require such
deft handling, and why we store them so carefully.

19.VI.99

Dummy

A man with a dummy goes from table to table along the waterfront.
The dummy asks people for money in a querulous, tinny voice.
Some give a little, some a lot. The man is very apologetic,
he sweats in the sun, his jacket is soaked between the shoulderblades.
With the hand not holding the dummy he wipes his bald forehead
constantly with a plaid handkerchief. People look at him blankly
as they hand the dummy its money. The dummy wears a tuxedo
and a beanie. Fiddlers and accordionists
and the hawkers of combs and mums and lighters fall
silent and draw back when the dummy comes demanding.

20.VI.99

Crowd Control

At the edge of town whole families plash like seals
on the lip of the sea. A child digs sand in handfuls
from the beach and flings it into the water. The waves
keep smoothing everything. Groups of mostly naked people
stand around gossiping, now and then one sits down
to cool off and stands up dripping. A father flings his son
over and over into the air. The young parade, the old paddle.
On a bench beside the beach, a man in a suit,
a man in a suit and tie,
and beside the bench, a sign: Forbidden the Swimming of Dogs.

20.VI.99

Sorites

The use of the moon is unknown. The weight of the moon
is negligible. The light of the moon guides the evolution of moths.
The evolution of anxiety has never ceased nor hesitated.
The anxiety of moths is palpable and strict. Start again.
The moon rises during the day so as to see what is going on.
Start again. O moon—he begins—o moon…
The difference between the moon at night and the moon during the day
is the whole measure of the brilliance of the sky. The measure
of what is lost in a day with no moon
is the weight of the moth's wing
to the moth.

20.VI.99

The Apotheosis

The lamb in the window has arrived at the height of self-absorption.
Like an invalid whom everything bothers, everything bores except illness,
it has perfected concentration on an ideal. Divested
of that greasy burr-clotted fleece its soul approaches spotlessness
like the sheet of slick paper under its high-hung head,
only five or six small gouts. And occasions of sin diminish swiftly.
Its heart is pure and empty, at hand in a small bowl.
A woman stops to admire the lamb—more than admire, to contemplate
its forthcoming transfiguration over a softly flickering bed of coals
and subsequent transubstantiation into her large family.

21.VI.99

Doves

Twenty-three doves stand calmly on the top wire,
every variety of coloration the island knows, from classic white
through ur-beige to banded and mottled anyhow.
Below them on the third wire of five, four sparrows fidget.
Suddenly, wings snapping, a report like a small gun, the doves
leap into the air together. A minute of panic, baseless
to judge from their ready settling back on the same wire, same
catalogue positions, but too much for the sparrows, who flee.
A good shot could pick off twenty-two in half an hour
before the last one caught on, but it would be demeaning.

21.VI.99

Planning

At the harbor all the passengers who are not yet passengers
inhabit the benches as slowly as they can, they comb their hair,
refold newspapers and eat nuts. Acres of concrete reflect the sun.
A boat comes in, but it's only a fishing boat, nets half-full of creatures
beyond boredom. The wind picks up, dies down, for the sake of incident.
Should a startling juxtaposition, a telling counterpoint, come in?
But the boat still isn't here and fancying doesn't bring it, not talk
nor narrative serendipity. No—he says—what brings the boat eventually
will be cooperative enterprise, to construct clocks, to define sea-lanes,
to organize ticket-sellers and second mates and underwriters
and yes, loads of people to sit around providing expectation.
The dreams prancing behind their vacant stares are of no account.

21.VI.99

The Octopus

Midsummer night: the sea has so little energy for speech,
sunset leaves it just goose-pimpled, pink and green.
What's under? sleepless fish, never-endingly-waving seaferns,
starfish that print themselves across sand and then sink in with no trace,
and octopus: the one that one stormy day wove between rocks,
unwinding and winding itself in under the rocks, its head
a sloppy pouch full of brain and calm eyes. It's down there now no doubt,
dancing slowly tip by tentacle-tip over fern-topped rock,
in the sun that can hardly quit today, even through water,
that will go down, soon, for a while behind the sea and come up
earlier than ever behind things and go looking among rocks
for the octopus, whose gaze swivels and marvels, just as the sea,
revealing whatever wants to be revealed, goes anywhere the sun says.

21.VI.99

A Vocation

In a row the baker lays out the loaves to rise in the dark
under their coverlets of cheesecloth like babies in bassinets
or the first tidying after a massacre. The baker leaves
for his small sleep and the cat comes in to count the loaves
and to pray disinterestedly for their ascension. Her meditation
is on the mice whose susurrus inside the ceiling
and back of the bales of paper behind the furnace
and along the narrow alleys in walls
reminds her of the sea, or rather when she hears the sea,
sotto voce, it reminds her of mice. She thinks
it's the sound that helps the moonlit sea to rise.
In the miracle, the bread the dead resemble multiplies.

22.VI.99

The Disappearance

In the first half-light the walkway is a thoroughfare of snails.
The front of the house has ten ascending like an affliction,
a nervous condition. All the snails are in a terrible hurry
to get where they're going before the sun can sauté them in the shell,
it seems impossible that any destination, however unsuitable,
can be close enough for their glacial haste to suffice. Catastrophe.
By eight o'clock they're all gone, not a sign
except four empty shells stuck to rocks and windowsills.
And while we're at it—he says—where do all the coathangers go?
The laundry sends home five or six a week and you can never find one.
It's the same thing, a miracle of nature, beyond human comprehension.

22.VI.99

Plot

On the low wall in front of the house, nine, ten,
eleven pots of starting flowering plants and then
a large oval stone with interesting pits, and then one more
pot. Or is it the other way around? Is this a question
for the gardener who set them out (all but the rock
which was already in place, with its interesting pits)
but probably without even counting? For the leisured
observer? yes but from which side, the house, the road,
and from which end, like Greek, like Hebrew? Or
can such a question be meaningless
at the same time that it is unavoidable?
It's enough—he says—to make you smash them all.

22.VI.99

In the Hands of the Breezes

In the hands of the breezes doors all over the house
open and close in turn, at random, swaying slightly
or slamming with a final report: nothing. The breezes seem
to want something they can't find, can't even remember,
and they search the same corners over and over, trying,
moving light things around in the same eddies, dust-
cats and dust-mice, a receipt from the pharmacy, a petal
blown in from the bougainvillea, the vine the breezes shake feebly,
futilely, not knowing what question to ask.

23.VI.99

Visible End

The pile of cut brush by the garden wall. The secret of the martyr
woven into the shroud. The wires hung from pole to pole with no
visible end. The stone centered on the pier. The hour
fastened to the four corners of the table. The hand on the table,
closed, its back in the air. The dog led down the road by odors.
The mention of a certain name. The four feet of the chair.
The station of the sun over the clock tower. The air
entrained by all the rest of the air, more than a fish in school,
more than a cormorant in the dotted line of an arrow.
The arrow, halfway past
halfway there.

23.VI.99

Not One

The two—he says—are distinct and inseparable
like the color and the motion of an olive grove
or the pitch and timbre of a voice lingering over a name,
not like sky and sea on a hazy day when islands
and boats seem to float in a false position. Sometimes—he says—
they overlap like the two hands in the lap of an old woman in church
or the thought and word and deed of an honorable man,
not like fig leaves over the first offenders' suddenly private parts.
Never, though, are they one, any more than your two feet,
or your flesh and blood.

23.VI.99

On the Beach

The dog lies sleeping on the beach in the late afternoon, waves
thrashing uphill nearly to her nose. She starts awake
at a bit of blown plastic, settles back
with concentrated attention on her face. She is dreaming
of flying, borne over the seaspray, legs ever on the stretch.
She dreams she is a ship, the very good ship Dog, with a crew of men
to caulk and trim her daily. She dreams the sea is a cat, a very
large cat, better ignored, fortunately confined. On the beach
the noise is amazing, waves on waves, red light poring over them.

24.VI.99

The Stones

Cicadas shout over notable stones. On one sits an old man
in the shade of a pine, smoking a pipe. Beside him on the ground
an empty bag of blue cloth. On the other side of him
his small black dog waits in the cool dust. The shade of the tree
shifts, if you wait long enough to notice again. In front of him
and his dog, a road, across the road a house, inside the house
a noise of four people arguing. The stones
are written on like pages, with the names of people who,
whatever else may be said of them, are dead.
Over the noise, the cicadas, ancient, incessant.

24.VI.99

Unaccountable

The heart of man—he says—is a mailbox dying of curiosity.
The soul entrusts it with the inscrutable. Our own houses
stand agape at our audacity. We baffle the sea.
Everything the hand of man lets fall is perfectly unlike
everything other, even and especially when made in imitation.
We astounded the gods when we had gods. Every day—he says—
I surprise myself, don't you? Look at these books, this garden,
that cannon in the square under the marble soldier.

24.VI.99

The Mission

Keys on the same chain disagree about home.
They clash at every step. Their picture of themselves
is exact and exclusive. In the dark
they consort with trash—hard coins and crumpled bills,
a headless match, cap of a pen, all the aimless,
vague stuff stuffed in there without plan or order…
Drawn forth in a fascicle a dozen times a day,
once in the light, of the many called one chosen,
thrusting where it belongs to be, that the tumblers fall
so… Locking or opening—this is a thing
for others to torment themselves about.

25.VI.99

Crocodile

The boy on the back of the motorbike clutches in one hand
a green inflated crocodile as big as he is, upright, with handles,
and his father in the other. Wind whistles through the beast's teeth.
The swallows darting over the road veer off sharply.
The very sea reels in terror, or mock terror, it doesn't
signify. The earth rolls backward under the wheels like anything.
And the dog that took out after them, the prize of its young life,
recedes, no bigger than a mouse, and then a flea.

25.VI.99

Egg Salad

What a destiny—he says—for an embryo: all set
to become a hen, a rooster, who knows, filched and bundled
with eleven more in a paper sack; subjected to terminal
thermal insult, roiling heat first then running cold; opened
flake by flake to the light like the soul of a prophet;
then diced in a low bowl; mashed; bound and thickened
with mayonnaise and a fierce forkful of mustard. Salt.
A life too strange for plot, a death too delicious for words.

25.VI.99

Colossus

Between two fingers of the hand outstretched a star.
Between the next the paring of a moon. Next, night.
The palm is full of light. The arm a dark road that goes home.
The prominences of the body overflow with brightness
and its recesses give brightness places to go still.
The feet grip down on rock, balancing, balancing.
When the face turns to face north it meets the wind
riding, massed, down from the mountains, and the eye
only blinks. One thin cloud hangs from the roof
and the whole cave of the world is filled
with the commentary of the sea.

26.VI.99

Ticket

I love the moment at the ticket window—he says—
when you are to say the name of your destination, and realize
that you could say anything, the man at the counter
will believe you, the woman at the counter
would never say No, that isn't where you're going,
you're going where you always go. Or to be sure
you could buy a ticket for one place and go to another,
less far along the same line. Suddenly you would find yourself
— he says—in a locality you've never seen before,
where no one has ever seen you and you could say your name
was anything you like, nobody would say No,
that isn't you, this is who you are. It thrills me every day.

26.VI.99

South

A man standing by the road holds an open map. The road
winds one way and the other. The land billows up behind him
and in front of him unrolls down to sea. He turns the map around,
reading, glancing left along the road and right. The sun stands overhead.
He's on an island, he begins with that. Maybe the map
is of some other island, though the sea looks familiar. This road
might be the red one here, or on the other side of that black name of a hill,
it might connect just around this curve (or that one, or either next)
with the road he's supposed to be on. He's on an island,
he ends with that, stuffing the map in his pack and turning
left.

26.VI.99

The Collector

Down among the fishcrates and plastic bottles, among the searocks,
down among splintered bamboo and mayonnaise caps and cuttlebones,
there have to be—he said—statistically speaking
the tailbones of a mermaid; whitening daintily,
curved and socketed like intaglio in ivory. They lie still linked
in a crevice between these yellow blocks of shattered cliff. I know it, I can
see it, and I search. And nobody—he said—
nobody else will stick to it long enough.

26.VI.99

On the Rack

On their rack the pens dream of books, love letters,
wills and deeds of gift, contracts and constitutions,
treatises on the ethics of individuality, analytical grammars,
handbooks on chirography, IOUs, guest lists, class notes…
It is time to wake but the shop is still dark, they panic
and cry out to the books on the tall shelves behind them.
But the books are entoiled in their own struggles
each with the recurring dream of its destiny. Soon the air
in the whole place reeks of despair, the walls seep,
the ceiling is a nest of tangled catatonic horror. After eons
the sun enters and the owner and the shutters rise, the door
is flung back at last and the calm business of day begins.

27.VI.99

Clear

Clear as the sea here is—he says—it's hard to see
what people are doing with their nether limbs,
and this is the first origin of the mermaids; though afterwards
they learned to lay eggs of themselves, like frogs, large single eggs
that hatch out on the sea foam in the sun, the hair already
flowing-long on the nymph as on the fully formed imago.
A man in the next village had one of these eggs—out of water
they perish and are preserved—and it was half-clear
like amber. Unfortunately it was destroyed during the war.
But I myself—he says—have heard them calling
as I lay at sea at night under the deck of my nodding boat.

27.VI.99

Corner

She moves down the rows of her long shop,
turning and watering, trimming and fluffing up,
naming her charges in a Latin long grafted on Greek,
and comes to a tremendous scarlet blossom
sprung from the corner of a green barrel
like a cloche on the head of a Martian, she says.
Desert succulents—she bursts out—that's all we are,
desert succulents, half thorns,
we store up, we store up, and once a year we wave these
frantic signals at all the pollinators in the world.

27.VI.99

Piece by Piece

He knows the house (his father lived there), and the bicycle
leaning against it was his own as a boy; and the hat
hanging from the handlebar he gave to a woman long ago
(she was bitter, he remembers, and refused to wear it). It all makes sense
piece by piece. But little by little his alarm deepens.
Why would someone put these things together? Who could do it?
When was he brought here? to see it? He knows
if he opens the door his first dog will be standing in the hall
and his mother's robe will be slung over a kitchen chair
and the clothesline and the footstool and the hunting knife
will be in the bathroom, and he turns and begins running
down the street he is about to recognize.

27.VI.99

Along the Coast

All day the stairs go down to the sea,
and people follow them. But at night
the stairs come up from the water, so as to be in place for morning,
and the others come up them, hesitant, silent, faint,
to move through streets dim with starlight, past the stalls
empty of cucumbers and roosters, around the corner of the square
where no one is selling film or gum or advice based on coffee grounds,
down the lane past the dark church, all night,
until with a great sigh the sun announces itself
and the steps pause for a moment and are at our disposal.

28.VI.99

The Cloth Bag

The old man with the cloth bag comes into the kitchen
from another room and sets an ornate inkstand on the table,
he shuffles out the outside door. In a while he comes back
with a handful of flight feathers—crow, gull, eagle, stork —
and puts them on the table. He goes out, comes back, empties his bag:
a fallen small nest, skull of a hedgehog, stone of four colors,
pair of turret shells with mirrorimage twists.
He sits down and watches the mess on the table. Evening falls,
night falls, a woman comes in and lights a lantern and leaves.
Suddenly he seizes the stone and flings it out the window,
blows out the lantern and goes away to bed.

28.VI.99

Line of Duty

Two men are fetching goods out of a truck parked on the front street,
a desk, a chest of drawers, a credenza, twelve high-backed chairs,
a typecase, a box of cabbages, wreathes, a green pony cart and a red one,
a hatrack full of helmets, a brazier filled with burning coals, a string bass,
a brace of hounds, a dolphin in a tank on wheels…
When they lead a small hippopotamus down the ramp the policeman
comes over to demand their papers. While the three men argue
smoke and hisses begin rising from the joints of the truck body
and from under the undercarriage comes an increasing drizzle of blood.
By the time they notice, the truck is on the point of exploding,
which it does with huge light and no sound. The two men run away
and the policeman sees that the town has gone gray and papery,
and at its edge the sea has quite stopped moving.

28.VI.99

The Mountain in the Middle

The mountain in the middle could be watching
all its children from brim to brim, fishing, bargaining,
making rolls and change and babies, swatting goats,
and the goats, the bees, the boats, the trees, all the perched churches,
the chalky limestone north and pumice south, the lesser crags,
the seven valleys in their loveliness, out to its own
very fringes which the wavelets lick—but the mountain
instead leans back its head in the sun
and loses in the blue its rapt gaze.

29.VI.99

Offering

The salt is on the table, and in the bread, and in every mouthful of sea.
Salt glistens among rocks above high tide, it stings
in the eyes of the divers and the bites of insects, it sticks
skin to skin in siesta and films every seaward surface of glass.
Its savor is in no danger, its word is on every tongue.
On the hills the goats lick it from their own coats.
It tans the hides of the old, beginning when they're young.
Here's a good pinch—he said—take it,
rub it between your fingers, rub it into your palm with your thumb,
blow it into the air, it sparkles all the way to the ground.
That's what nobody can live without.

29.VI.99

Outdoor Theater

On the whitewashed wall of the house behind the ticket booth
the film flickered, less after dark. The sound dinned. The Big Dipper
hung over the wall like a sign for Exit, or the Gents'. The perfect touch
—he says—is that that house behind has a pen for fowl
and in the midst of big taut dialogue (I think she was asking
why he must volunteer) the turkey let out great spitty strings of gobble.
I couldn't get over the creature's timing. But just when he dies—he says—
the hero I mean, a meteor streaked by, right through the Dipper's bowl.

29.VI.99

History

His day is written on his clothes—the sliver
of mimosa flower from by the garden wall stuck in his sleeve
where he brushed past on his way to the garage, the spot
of chocolate on his cuff from lunch, the three burrs
from after lunch on the hill behind the village on his butt,
the tide-marks of sweat-salt, high and low.
Tomorrow, again. But tonight
all his years will come in, in force, in earnest, out of order.

30.VI.99

New Mown

The new-cut and -baled hay is stacked into walls,
golden and tall on the edge of the golden field.
They make a house, the mark of a house, as much or more
than some of the oldest traceable in the hills. The field is giving back
so much light to the morning it seems a saint of gratitude.
Nobody lives here—he says—nobody works these lands.
Yesterday this field was scrub. The people from the hills,
the old people, come here or near here, they harvest, build,
just one day. But yes, there's a man with a truck
who comes and finds the hay and hauls it home.
He's always done it, and his father before that.

30.VI.99

Faculties

The empty drawer in the chest standing three-legged beside the road
hangs out in the sun, filling slowly. It smells of camphor
and salt. The other drawers are closed, one locked. Junk.
The wood inside the open drawer, color of dry grass, color of summer,
has begun to recall so well how it felt to be a branch
that a sparrow flits down to perch, to peek inside with one eye.
Under the chest, in shade a cat waits. The sparrow knows.
Slowly the stuff in the other drawers is forgetting everything.

1.VII.99

Stepwise

Right hand steadies itself on rock, rock rests
harder on ledge, ledge leans back
that much more on mountain. Left foot feels
for step, instep curls into place, pressed
into mountain. Eye fixes everything
one at a time. Time steps
delicately over stones,
leading. Goat-time, bell-time.
The sun herds it. Left hand, shielding,
frees the eyes from time to time for horizon,
which circles, excited like a dog but
at the speed of light.

1.VII.99

A Certain Hour

At a certain hour the sun
quite tightly yet so gently hardly a hair's betrayed
grasps the back of the neck and dismounts the skull. The brain,
like a cat of any age plucked by the scruff, entranced,
suffused, forgets the elaborations scheduled by its proprietor
and becomes an intimate of the day, which is enormous, of great depth
and total certainty. So loudly that it bypasses the ear entirely,
the sun speaks its one tremendously long word into the manifold
folds of the brain so that they exfoliate
like the elephant's fan of ear or the photon sail of a hypership,
a square meter of concentration. For a moment
everything is quite, quite clear. Then while the sun averts its gaze
behind a momentary cloud, the brain repacks itself and assumes
some of its former dignity, the regalia of its intent.

1.VII.99

Philippic and/or Jeremiad

Old man walking, looking down, stops and peers,
looks around him once then bends far down:
one of the island's venerable, militant ants hefting a thorn
the length of a finger, titanic. Old man glances forward,
sees easily where the ant is going (line of ants; hole),
looks around again to see if anyone's watching,
picks up the thorn between thumb and finger, ant still attached
(legs groping) and carries it near the goal. Sets it down.
Straightens up. The ant drops the thorn; runs off; runs back;
runs around it; seizes the thorn again and struggles off
in another direction. Old man shakes head, sighs,
wanders off formulating, formulating, formulating.

2.VII.99

The Message

Someone has written it, certainly. And someone,
someone else, has folded it and tossed it aside,
and it has fetched up in this bush. Not a thorn bush.
A spider has spun an especially elaborate web above it.
Still a nonarachnophobe could come, reach in for it,
pull it out of its net of twigs (sharp, but not thorns).
Maybe nothing is worth all that. Maybe no message
says much more, retrieved and unfolded, than this.

2.VII.99

Libation

The clean-up man has come into his hour, his own
because everyone else has left it. He carries the tables into the back
and piles the chairs on them, opening the whole front to the sidewalk;
and there with his reiterate broom, little by little,
he causes to accumulate, or he accumulates,
what others dispersed. He won't look until he's finished,
until he's restored the chairs and tables, until the moon has set.
Under the last lamp he has left lit, he pores
over the fruits of his work: the seventy-nine cigarette butts
and six whole cigarettes; the three coins and a small bill folded in thirds;
the tickets for the boat, all cancelled; both halves of a torn map.
One good push and it's all down the gutter, except the bill and cigarettes
and two of the coins.

3.VII.99

Levels

Up over the night road the transformer
crackles and hums to itself, furious in the dark,
crucified to its tall pole, crammed with zeal. Higher,
on the big disk at the top the town contributes, a pair of storks,
perplexing, way too late to mate, perch anyway. Above the storks, the stars.
The transformer, a creature all compound of grudge,
a pair of birds who might as well be on vacation,
this imponderable strew of stars—he says —
what do we expect, daylight beasts with no knack for it?
Forget it, this is a ship without a pilot.

3.VII.99

Syzygy

Rain and the idea of rain stroll arm in arm up the coast.
Who cares what anybody thinks? They could tear off
their different kinds of clothes and leap into the sea,
disporting. They could lie down together in a church.
If they were made they were made for each other. If they had families
their families would bury idols to put them right. Under the moon's light
the sea lies under their conjoined ministrations calmed,
all its larger projects dissolved in their millioning.
They love each other more perfectly than you. They have
no secret, they are a secret. No one can see them both at the same time.

3.VII.99

Order in Disorder

From one table after another stare the same woman and boy
in the same blank-faced postures denoting grief suspended,
over the same caption in three or four languages. On paper
what surrounds them varies, in differing maelstroms they stand still
staring. Gulls feint and squabble among the awnings,
the tops of masts nod like a forest of violin bows,
the intratabular and intertabular diplomacy of the waterfront
is constructive, is promising, and the woman and the boy
stare together past the glances of people and gulls into the white sky.

4.VII.99

The Responsibility

It wasn't what we planned—she says—but we have it here, stiff
and accusatory, as if it were ours or our fault. We have it
arms and legs and all, and these few clothes for it, which we can't
get it into. We should leave it outside until it behaves better.
We have a name for it on this paper. We don't see the use of it, nor do
the children any more. The people across the road have one too,
what are things coming toward? We found a box almost big enough,
if we could fold it up. There's a space behind the lemon tree maybe
big enough for the box. They gave us time, till evening. The children
are tired of playing with it, they go off to touch the butts
of the soldiers' rifles and run away. The soldiers are all right, they're older.

4.VII.99

Stay

Under the walls the dead. Under the dreams
dreams of the dead. Over the far hill
the acid, purifying light of early morning.
Taste in the mouth of stale time, still.
In the long brick shed the sheep and chickens
stay legs folded gazing quietly through the air.
The dead lie under our walls to hold them up.
What would we do without them? We'll never know.
The animals, snug, know better than to build.

6.VII.99

The Door

A door from somewhere, off its hinges, across trestles for painting,
its knocker tilted up to keep out of it, handle a green
brass island in the fresh brown, glares with what authority it can
under the circumstances at the impertinent open sky.
The idea that anyone can be on either side of it
makes it sweat. As for the jamb left to its own
totally naive devices, the thought is not to be endured.
The street in front of the door empties for a few hours,
fills again for the evening bustle, all those shoes tap by,
and no one all night will knock.

6.VII.99

Tide Pool

Above high water, where one long wave washed it,
a crab in its few inches draped with spare weed
is not moving, won't move even prodded. But no—he says —
not stubborn any more than your great-grandfather is stubborn.
If you felt the water you'd understand, sun's cooked it through.
Tell this to that son-in-law of mine. And look here
next to it—he says—on the rock where the water's gone off completely,
this butterfly spread out like a shop window, stiff as a tiny board,
right where it took its last drink. It was one of those big yellow ones
but the salt has leached it white, more than white, almost clear.

6.VII.99

The Sands

A woman lies on the rocks, counting. When she gets to six hundred
she'll turn onto her back. Just after two thousand
she'll open her book and pretend to read until the others go away again.
Around twenty thousand night will fall and the stars
come out, one by one, as from the twentieth to the twenty-first million
snowflakes will drift down onto the highest peak behind her.
At every billion a bell tolls, until the last one. Meanwhile,
the fishes teem, the almond petals flourish and drop away,
and while the world spins under her, singing its one note,
the terrible gift gives itself over and over.

7.VII.99

Ready

The cedar weighs an extra hundred pounds with dew.
In a haze the hills are still half awake.
On the phone poles the crows practice the flap-and-caw,
and the wind runs its fingertips through everything tousled,
everything sleep-matted nor yet spruce for day.
The hedgehog doesn't count, just now bedded back down,
but the lizard, frozen on its already hot rock, stands prepared
to take on any demoiselle thrown at it, the old man
on the bench in the square has nearly made up his mind to walk,
and the butterflies are going crazy around each other over the oregano.

8.VII.99

Misplaced

The woman at the last table thumbs through an album:
the previous week: mountain, mountain, sunset, sunset, sunset,
friends, more friends, sea, sea, sea, goat, herd of goats,
man riding a horse off a cliff into the sea, sunset,
sea. She sighs and sets it down and sips her tea.
He's sitting at the next table, the next to last, his hair dripping
as it always will, as will his horse,
who stands nearby with baleful eyes,
but she avoids their gaze as deftly as the waiter.
It was only her camera, only a moment's notice…

8.VII.99

Glimpse

Sleep—sleep for such as us—he says —
is a page of words stretching in all directions
without end, although our ability to sample it,
nap by nap even over a whole life, is circumscribed.
The wonder is that any time we are set down on it
we are set down in a new place, or almost every time,
there's barely moment enough to figure out which way
the words are running before we're taken up again
like divers letting their last air buoy them back above,
yet we come back regularly with quite marvelous stories
gleaned in a glimpse. It is also striking to me—he says —
that though we hear from each other of familiar passages,
we almost never meet anyone there, except the dead.
I suppose it's just that there are so many more of them.

9.VII.99

Eight Greek Lyrics

Το Τηλεφώνημα

Ήθελα να μιλήσω στον πατέρα μου
ανάμεσα στους νεκρούς, μα ο τηλεφωνητής
είπε ότι θα μου στοίχιζε
όλα όσα είχα. Είχα

πολλά· μερικά βουνά, ένα καλέμι,
δυο μάτια διαφορετικά, το φως,
την περσινή χρονιά, το τέλος άσχημου
βήχα, το καύκαλο χελώνας, τις τσέπες μου,

τη γλώσσα της θάλασσας που'λεγε Όχι, Ναι,
δεκαεννέα υποσχέσεις. Κι είχα τηλέφωνο. Ρώτησα,
Όλα; Απάντησε, Όλα εκτός από
την ενοχή. Αυτήν θα χρειαστείς.

The Phone Call

I wanted to speak to my father
among the dead, but the operator
said it would cost me
all I had. I had

lots: some mountains, a chisel,
two disparate eyes, the light,
the past year, the end of an ugly
cough, a tortoise shell, my pockets,

the tongue of the sea that said No, Yes,
nineteen promises. And a telephone. I asked,
All? The answer: All except
the debt. That you will need.

Νεκρή φύση

Σε μια πλευρά του δρόμου, στο μπαλκόνι
τα πουκάμισά μας χωρίς κουρέματα
και τα εσώρρουχά μας χωρίς τα κομμάτια μας,
απ' τις τρίχες μας και τα λάδια μας
όλα καθαρισμένα, κρέμονταν

κοιτώντας με κενά μάτια. Στην άλλη πλευρά
κρέμονταν στο παράθυρο του κρεοπωλείου
ένα αρνί με το ολόγυμνο κεφάλι του
κι ένας χοίρος που κρατεί ακόμα
τα δυο χαριτωμένα αυτιά του.

Still Life

On the one side of the street, on the balcony
our shirts without haircuts
and our underwear without our parts,
of our tresses and oils
all cleansed, hang

staring with empty eyes. On the other side
hang in the window of the butcher's shop
a lamb with its stark-naked head
and a pig that still retains
his two shapely ears.

Ονειροκρίτης

Αν δείτε ότι βρίσκεται
στο χέρι σας η καρδιά του
πατέρα σας, και πως χτυπάει:
επιτυχία στη δουλειά.

Αν ονειρευτείτε μερμήγκια, θα
αντιμετωπίσετε
τους τοίχους, αξεπέραστους,
του τάφου σας. Μη φοβηθείτε.

Αν δείτε πως τον αριθμό
τον έσβησαν του σπιτιού σας
με ξυραφάκια, κι έγραψαν
καινούργια διεύθυνση εκεί,

θάναι προειδοποίηση
ότι θα ταξιδέψετε
στον Άδη· θα συναντήσετε
πρόσωπο που σας μισούσε.

Αν ότι ονειρεύεστε
ονειρευτείτε, πράγματι
το δεύτερο όνειρο θα βγει
πιο αληθινό απ' τη ζωή σας.

Στον ύπνο σας αν περπατάτε
σε δρόμο όλο στρωμένο με
διαμάντια, όμως δε μπορείτε
να τα μαζέψετε: το πρωί

σίγουρα θα πεθάνετε.
Και πρέπει να ξυπνήσετε.
Ή να μπείτε στο τρίτο όνειρο
τώρα με χέρια αδειανά.

Dreambook

If you see lying
in your hand the heart
of your father, and it beats:
success in work.

If you dream ants
you will confront
the walls, unscalable,
of your tomb. Don't fear.

If you see that the number
of your house has been erased
with razor-blades, and they have written
a new address there,

it will be a foretelling
that you will travel
to Hades; you will meet
a person who hated you.

If you dream that you are
dreaming, in fact
the second dream will turn out
truer than your life.

If in your sleep you walk
on a street all paved with
diamonds, yet you cannot
pick them up: in the morning

you will surely die.
And you must wake up.
Or enter the third dream
now, with open hands.

Ο Ράφτης ο μεθυσμένος

Τα πράγματα πρώτα είναι πράσινα,
έπειτα μαύρα· και τα δύο του
αρέσουν, όπως του αρέσει το μπλε,
κι οι ρίγες, οι κίσσες, και η ναφθαλίνη.
Το μυαλό του είναι όλο τρύπες,
τα βήματα του σαν αραιές βελονιές.
Είτε η αυγή δεν είναι κάθετη
είτε αυτός. Σύντομα θα ξηλώσει
το πεζοδρόμιο· θα το λυπηθεί.
Επηρεάζεται από αστέρες
κι ίσκιους. Προσπαθεί να κατουρήσει
ένα σκυλί, που φεύγει τρέχοντας·
κατουράει ένα ποδήλατο, που σκούζει.
Χωρίς δάχτυλα, σκέφτεται, το χέρι
θαναι κουτάλι. Η γυναίκα του
το άκουγε αυτό πολλές φορές, και ξέρει.
Αυτή κεντάει—κεντήματα τα πιό
περίπλοκα—με μικροσκοπική
βελόνα—έναν άνδρα ανάποδα·
σε λάβαρο πάνω απ' το κεφάλι του:
Αν τον δεις να ιππεύει με μπαμπου-
μπαστούνι, λέγε, Γειά του αλόγου σου.

The Drunken Tailor

First things are green,
then black; both
please him, as he's pleased by blue,
and stripes, magpies and mothballs.
His mind is all holes,
his steps like loose stitches.
Either the dawn is not vertical
or he. Soon he will unzip
the sidewalk; he will regret it.
He is influenced by stars
and shadows. He tries to piss
on a dog, which runs off;
he pisses on a bicycle, which screams.
Without fingers, he thinks, *the hand*
would be a spoon. His wife
has heard this many times, and knows.
She embroiders—embroidery most
intricate—with a microscopical
needle—a man, backwards;
on a banner over his head:
If you see him riding on a bamboo
cane, say, Good health to your horse.

Κατάσταση

Τα γυαλιά του είναι κάπου—όχι εδώ,
ούτε επάνω στο κεφάλι του
ούτε κρεμασμένα στο λαιμό του
ούτε στο τραπέζι στην κουζίνα—
    ίσως εκεί

στο περβάζι, ή κάτω απ' την ελιά
πού η γάτα κοιμάται τυλιγμένη σαν
εκείνο το κουβάρι το γκρίζο φεγγάρι·
ή μακρύτερα, στα λιβάδια του
    πατέρα του.

Παντού θα ψάχνει στα λιβάδια, όλη
τη νύχτα, όπως έψαχνε κάθε νύχτα
για κάτι που δε μπορεί να θυμηθεί.
Ανησυχεί που ποτέ δε θα το βρει
    χωρίς γυαλιά.

Situation

His glasses are somewhere—not here,
neither on his head
nor hung around his neck
nor on the table in the kitchen —
     maybe there

on the windowsill, or underneath the olive
where the cat sleeps wrapped up like
that balloon the gray moon;
or farther, in the pasture of
     his father.

He'll search everywhere in the pasture, all
night as he has searched every night
for something he can't remember.
He worries that he will never find it
     without glasses.

Το Τραγούδι της ακρίδας

Γνώριζε εννέα τραγούδια η αρκούδα—
όλα για το μέλι

Μια φορά το φθινόπωρο μελέταγε
ο αρχαιολόγος για να μάθει αν
είχαν κάποιοι ανακατευτεί
με το βράχια του· πολλά
σπασμένα βρήκε, μερικά
φευγάτα. Ρώτησε
την άδεια αχλαδιά,
Τι έγινε 'δώ; Και με φωνή
όχι πιο δυνατή απ' τον άνεμο
του έδωσε την ιστορία
του τυμβωρύχου και της ακρίδας:

Πώς ήρθε άνθρωπος με ψηλές
μπότες και ράβδο· δεν ήθελε
μεγάλα πράματα,
δεν ήθελε τίποτα
το χρυσό ή το βαρύ·
έψαχνε μόνο το κλειδί
των εποχών· κι ερευνούσε τα
βάθη της γης μας με τη ράβδο του.
Κινούνταν σαν αρκούδα αλλά
κελαϊδούσε. Μα το άκουγε
κάπου το τραγούδι
της ακρίδας, ξανά, και ξανά,
ανάμεσα στις πέτρες,
εδώ ή εκεί· πέρα-δώθε
τον οδηγούσε το τραγούδι,
και προς τα μπρος
ώς το βράδυ το βαθύτερο, ώς και
του γιαλού το βάραθρο.

Ο αρχαιολόγος κουνήθηκε· είπε,
Εκείνο το γκρεμό;

The Song of the Grasshopper

Once came to study autumn
an archaeologist, to learn
if anyone had meddled
with its rocks; many
he found broken, several
fled. He asked
the empty pear tree,
What happened here? In a voice
no stronger than the wind
she gave him the story
of the grave-thief and the grasshopper:

How a man came with tall
boots and a staff; he wanted
no big thing,
he wanted nothing
golden or heavy;
he sought only the key
of the seasons; and he searched
to the depths of our earth with his staff.
He moved like a bear but
sang. But he heard it
somewhere, the song
of the grasshopper, again, again,
among the stones,
here or there; roundabout
the song led him,
and onwards
into the evening, deeper, as far
as the shore's precipice.

The archaeologist stirred; he said,
That cliff?

Παίξανε αύρες πάνω από
τα ζεστά βράχια· χαμήλωνε
ο ήλιος κι έβγαινε πιο
λαμπρά το φεγγάρι.
Όμως δεν έχεις—
είπε—τ' αχλάδια—;
Κι είπε αυτή—Μα θα τα 'χω.

Breezes played over
the warmed rocks; the sun
sank and out came the more
brightly the moon.
Yet you don't have —
he said—pears?
And she: But I will have.

Στη Παλιά θέση

Σήμερα χιόνι, όχι όλη τη μέρα
μα ημέρα για μπότες. Ο άνεμος
σφυρίζει απόψε στις γωνίες
της στέγης. Ο γιος κοιμάται
στο πάνω πάτωμα· στη γυναίκα απούσα
ακόμη τηλεφώνησα. Δεν κοιμάται

το σπίτι, περιμένει την αυγή
με αταραξία εκπληκτική
σαν βουδας απ' ασβεστόλιθο.
Πότε θα μάθω έτσι να περιμένω;
Ξαφνικά κακαρίζει ο πετεινός
που δραπέτεψε πέρσι στην αυλή μας

παράλογα νωρίς, όπως συνήθως.
Περνάνε πάλι τα πατώματα
πόρτα-πόρτα αυτές οι μπότες.
Όταν ολοκαίνουργη ήταν η γη
πού πήγε ο άνεμος
να μάθει τ'όνομά του;

In the Old Place

Today snow, not all day
but a day for boots. The wind
whistles at evening in the corners
of the roof. The son sleeps
on the upper floor; the woman, away,
I've already phoned. It doesn't sleep,

the house, it awaits dawn
with astonishing composure
like a buddha of limestone.
When will I learn to wait that way?
Suddenly the rooster crows
who escaped last year into our yard—

absurd, early, as usual.
They pass again over the floors
door to door, these boots.
When the earth was totally new
where did the wind go
to learn its name?

Νησί

Αν είχαμε λιμάνι
αν είχαμε δωμάτια κοντά
αν στους τοίχους τους κρέμονταν πίνακες
αν οι πίνακες έδειχναν λιμάνια
γιατί να δείχνουν άλλο λιμάνι
από το δικό μας;
                    Σ'έναν άλλο τόπο
άκουγα να ρωτάνε γιατί
οι πίνακες στους τοίχους των δωματίων
να δείχνουν το μέρος
όπου βρίσκονται, αφού ήταν
κιόλας εκεί· ένας ήταν αυτοί
ψηλός λαός, λιανός από
το τρέξιμο, για το τρέξιμο.

Αφού τελείωσα
γύρισα 'δώ.

Island

If we have a harbor
if we have rooms for rent nearby
if paintings hang on the walls of the rooms
if they are paintings of harbors
why should they be paintings of harbors
other than ours?
                    In another place
we have heard them ask why
paintings on the walls of rooms should be of
where they are when they are
there already; they were
a tall people lean with running
for the sake of it.

When we finished what we went for we came back.

Where Am I

Aigina, an island of 83 square kilometers in the Saronic Gulf, which is an arm of the Aegean arm of the Mediterranean Sea, lies about 30 kilometers from Epidaurus (west), the Corinth Canal (northwest), and Piraeus, the port of Athens (northeast). Before Athens' heyday Aigina competed as a political and naval center. It brought to Greece the Persian concept of money: silver nugget-coins embossed with a sea turtle, bright punctuation for museum cases. Halfway to the present, the port's people, forced inland by Barbarossa's devastation, settled the hill they now, two centuries after the redoubt was abandoned again, call Paleochora, Old Town, quiet with ruins and upkept chapels. Aigina spent a few years after 1820 as first capital of the new nation. It specializes in the growing of pistachios and the accommodation of summering Athenians.

*   *   *

After describing the shape of the island—roughly triangular, and among triangles roughly equilateral—its historian Stamatis says (in Greek), "Maybe this form was to be symbolized by the 'triskelida' figure on the ancient Aeginetan coins." (Obverse of the turtle?) The conjecture presumes recognition of the island's general shape long preceding any actual map. The question is, how does one realize that one lives on a more-or-less triangle? It is visually evident from no point on the island, including the summit of Oros (532 meters). From there—the point where Aeacus, besought by drought-stricken citizens, petitioned his father for rain—the sea is visible on all sides, but it remains impossible to distill from the complexities of coast and contour the more-than-godlike perspective of a map. It's a beautiful mess down there.

One might learn quickly enough that one can (only) *go around* the island, which is what "island" means to a person on it, and also, differently, to a sailor skirting its coast. Walking the ins and outs of bays and capes, recalling sailors' talk, one would arrive at the first-order generalization *self-contained*, aware of moving either clockwise or counterclockwise, or rather (this antedates clocks) deasil or widdershins, directions more immediate for island dwellers than compass points or (compasses too) the apparently single-minded career of the Sun, whose chariot plunges across while I go round and round; and discover, despite the senses' endless record of detail, the shore as a closed curve. Any island is a circle. One could have lived many kinds of lives on it with no more exact image of its larger shape. (How bizarre, conversely, to begin, foreign, with the shape before setting foot on the island.)

What further experiences suffice to produce the impression, not of a rough circle, but of an equilateral triangle? Suppose me an especially restless islander: walking enough times around this promontory, I realize (1) that it's quite a sharp turn and (2) that there are no others comparably sharp for quite a while. The promontory becomes a turn beyond other turns; the segments preceding and following it become straight lines. At another level of generalization, the third by my count, I recollect only a few other such turns on the island—two. At this point each becomes an apex and the island a triangle. Refinement to the next stage—walking one side takes roughly as many steps as walking another—is not conceptually difficult, though differences in the topography of the sides complicate it immeasurably. The Chinese reputedly used different miles for uphill and downhill.

What's remarkable and forgettable is how very long it would take to arrive at these sensible conclusions, obvious from the map. One person, in even a short lifetime—if she or he did nothing else, such as gathering roots or herding goats or plowing, and nothing prevented ubiquitous access, such as hostile orchardists on coastal plains or big dogs on mountain farms, and topography offered no insurmountable obstacles to circumnavigation, such as headlands steep enough to rebuff all but conjecture about their coastal shape, as in the whole southeast limb of Aigina—could discover it all.

But the person would have to have formed a desire to know the shape of the island. This desire is difficult to account for before maps make that kind of idea about the shapes of places a commonplace. In the absence of desire knowledge would arise slowly, percepts reiterated often enough to find their way into consciousness by chance. Or precepts, to carry it across generations.

Contemplating the question *How long is the coast of Britain?* led Benoit Mandelbrot to invent fractal geometry. (It depends how long your ruler is; infinitely, is one answer.)

*   *   *

Though Honda makes one too, I sing the Yamaha Mate 50. The engine is a thirtieth the size of a freeway hawg's but geared to climb like a squirrel. If it won't go everywhere feet could, it enjoys paths no sane person would attempt in a car, though I have seen cars on them. It will carry a Greek family of four plus a hatrack. It keeps running in rain too thick to see through, fits neatly inside the hatch of a ferry, likes a sip of gasoline every few days, creates refreshing breezes out of thin air, knows its way home in the dark.

*   *   *

Among mappings, the name:

    Aigina   Aegina   Egine   Égine   Egina   Aegine

all derived by hook or crook from the sound of the Greek and the difficulty of transliterating words from the Greek alphabet (by certain criteria the first invented, and the last.) The 'g' is often rendered as 'y' in names such as Iphiyenia, Yannis. Each transliteration proliferates into pronunciations, the written sign both resulting from and causing confusion. Pronunciations vary with the speaker's native language: the French tourist's "Égine" and the English one's "Aegina" share no phonetic features but the 'n' and possibly the vowel preceding it. Where is the island's name?

Surely in the mouths of its inhabitants. But that would include the name used by an internet service provider celebrating the introduction of touch-tone dialing to this area code: "It's a great step for all of 0297." Zero Two Nine Seven includes the outlying island of Agistri (Angistri). It would include the outlying island of Moni ("Careful how you pronounce that!" says a jocular Greek friend) if there were anyone living on Moni, or any telephone.

*   *   *

Some notes, from hundreds in my inebriated head, on the maps of Aegina. [Review in detail the five commercially available. Note Stamatis cribbing one. Others' maps: Thompson's great impermanent portolan/ songlines in his walking guide; Yannoulis' in tourist book; my rallye sketch, motorcycle times among key points, drawn I think from memory. Speculate: if really rich person wanted one, what would goddamn decent topographic map of the island (US Geologic Survey 7.5 ' series) cost? Recall best though outdated map hung in a few hotels, said to have been caused to be produced by army general who lived on island—Petriti, of World War II and the road sign? No evidence.]

The audience to whom the five different tourist maps are sold is land-attached. Every waterfront store and stall in the four ports carries one or more of these blurry, lurid, foldout portraits. A roadmap is a set of suggested experiences: dodgy business. All but one omit the road, finished years ago, connecting Portes on the southeast to the high inland road that skirts Oros, though without it nothing like a wheeled circumnavigation is possible. None of the maps helps someone exhaustively curious to determine which landscape item—one, say, of a splay of coves on the wild south coast—corresponds to which name. The map ("go here then there") is not only not the territory, but shoddy. The road designations "primary," "secondary," et. al., particularly encourage misrepresentation. On the best of the five maps the route down from Pachia Rachi to the shore at Marathonas just wriggles brightly a bit; on the ground it's drastic, not only in slope but in purely notional paving. Incomplete information? A wish to exaggerate progress? Inconsistent concepts of road-ness? A too-blithe embrace of the arbitrariness of all significations, such as confident lines and colors?

Water-directed maps, yachts' charts, are readily available and accurate. By local definition—ask in the market—all foreign boat people have money, though many of them feel that they don't, as the state of their teeth may testify. In any case their maps have to be right and their maps are right.

(If photography were easier—properties of silver and glass under special circumstances more readily understood—and had been invented three thousand years ago, would the project of mapping this world have developed differently? Would a map be a series of photographs, as the commonest record of a choreography is a video?)

Inhabitants don't need a map, don't think of wanting one, and often can't easily read one, or rather translate to it. In a ravine in the middle of the island I dismounted to ask two guys working on a power line whether as the map implied the hint of a trail up the far slope led to a certain village. To begin, I pointed to where we were. Guy looked at the map and pointed to a spot a mile away—"We are here." If I had pointed up the trail and spoken the village's name, he could have told me yes or no. He knew his island; I knew my map; so I was right; which didn't help me at all.

*   *   *

Brought up on triple-A and the *National Geographic*, I take for granted the mappedness of any place I'm likely to find myself in. As recently as 1940, according to *Encyclopedia Britannica*, "an appraisal by the U.S. Air Force indicated that… less than 10 percent of the world was mapped in sufficient detail for even the meagre requirements of pilot charts." The following five years did a great deal, in their curious way, to amend this deficit. Around the world many national mapping programs began from USAF data gathered before 1945.

Britannica on Maps and Surveying (sv. Mapmaking; Elements; Nomenclature) promises a gaudy *mise-en-abyme*:

> At the local levels, however, there are different kinds of problems. The larger scales of most basic topographic map series permit the naming of quite minor hilltops, ridges, streams, and branches, for which designations can be obtained locally. In sparsely settled country few names in actual use may be obtained for minor features, while in other areas inquiries may reveal inconsistencies and confusions in both spelling and application of local names. In some areas, for example, local residents may tend to refer to small streams by the name of the present occupant of the headwater area. The occupants of opposite sides of a mountain sometimes refer to it by different names. In coastal areas the waterman and landsman may use different references for the same features.

But the paragraph is organized as prelude to the happy ending of terminological globalization:

> A prime opportunity for resolving these problems is presented when a topographic map of an area is prepared for publication. By extensive inquiry and documentation and research of local records and deeds,

the appropriate form and application of nearly all names can be
determined.

Thereafter triumph will be swift and complete:

> Publication and distribution of the map as an official document may
> then tend to solidify local usage and eliminate the confusions that
> previously existed.

Isolated for scrutiny these declarations reveal not only an
encyclopedia's devotion to linguistic normalization but its circular pitfalls.
Differences in naming—between "waterman and landsman" or people
living on one or the other side of a mountain or at its base or farther
up its side— don't become "problems" until the mapmaker blows into
town demanding consensus. Their "solutions," perhaps majoritarian, are
adjudicated by the cartographic outsider.

The mapmaker's demand is worth privileging because a broader
view is better than a narrower one, all other things being equal, though
they never are. The sum of bewilderment in the universe may be
diminished when one thing comes to have fewer rather than more names,
but information about differences in people's experience is lost. Where do
the colliding names come from? Do seaward denizens name for weather
and landward for vegetation? What's the *story*? The decision among
alternatives is political: don't sing "Now it's Istanbul, not Constantinople…
that's nobody's business but the Turks'" in Athens, where 1453 is seared
into the national brain. Political too is the program of uniform naming,
conducted on behalf of some kind of totalizing power. A bank detests two
designations for its branch halfway up the mountain.

Oros—also one common noun for "mountain"—was Ellaniou Dia,
God of the Hellenes, when Aeacus stood at its crest and called down rain.
Later, like other summits, it became Profitis Elias (not profit but prophet),
who was assumed from a mountaintop; also Analipsys (Assumption).
Since peaks were once sacred to the sun, Elias may have gotten a boost
from Helios.

* * *

The name of the island, says Stamatis, "is in fact inexplicable and rare." Something confused about fertility, ants, and pigeons. One derivation makes it Phoenician for "Pigeon Island." As for the ants (ancient *murmex*), we have the story of Aeacus's request to his father Zeus to turn them into people because he was lonely, alone on the island, resulting in the Myrmidons led to battle by his grandson Achilles. The town has a Myrmidon Street. The ants of Aegina are not especially large, but strong and startlingly fast, with long legs that jack up the front end and brandish the mandibles something fierce. As for the generation between Achilles and his grandfather, better not to ask; one brother may be buried at the ancient naval harbor, a little north of the main port, near the single butter-brown Classical column featured on most postcards.

*   *   *

Early, before the sun's too high, I ride my Mate halfway up Oros, as far as road plausibly continues, which is also as far down as I've seen the huge, shaggy, brown half-wild goats, and walk the rest of the way, dry, rocky. At the top, the closet-sized chapel contemplates its arduous offerings, scrappy flowers and old pictures. From the rock that rises over it I can see southwest, pressed between horizontal masses of brilliant blue, the mountain where Troizen is, where Theseus was born, and, far around to the right, beyond the isthmus he cleared of robbers (Corinth and its canal lost in mist), Eleusis where Mary Renault has him wrestle to the death, and on to Athens where he came to be king and the unhappy father of kings, today like most days a brown smudge.

Step by step, I have been leaving behind one after another the island's daily sounds. The key to John Cage's career, half a century ago, came to him when he entered an anechoic chamber at Harvard (he tells the story in his first book *Silence*) and emerged to complain mildly that among the state-of-the-art acoustic baffles he had still heard two sounds, one high and one low. The engineer replied that the high sound was his nervous system at work, the low one the circulation of his blood.

*   *   *

I had an image of Livadia where Nikos Kazantzakis lived and worked (the word means "meadow") before I ever saw it, and even a fantasy of living in it. I arrive and find no "in" to it, no here here. His house, empty, on a treacherous coastal road not like a street, facing nothing except sea, stands half a kilometer up the coast from the one I inhabit. Houses sit here and there about as thick as a suburb. Nothing visible whatsoever distinguishes the village of Livadia from the village of Plakakia, the name I write for a return address. According to some maps the promontory where his house is located is still named Cape Livadia, or Cape Plakakia, but the village—the area—is now called Kazantzaki. Across the island, I follow a track as far as I can (big dogs) and wonder, am I in X? I don't know if I ever saw Vlachides. Houses yes, three in sight. The name is printed clearly here on this paper; everyone around knows the place; it's like being in seventh grade.

My feet understand how to get from my door to the market, the sea, the mountaintop. Language wants us to agree on names for things; cartographers are its fundamentalists. My Mate 50 chuckles beside the road while I study a new path from the foot of Paleochora to the temple of Aphaia.

Anyway Kant told us how this stuff occurs in a space all must conceive and none can occupy. I seem to stand here, or I remember standing there, seeing the skyline, the grouping of houses, the pistachio grove, hearing the magpie and the sea and the breath in my nose, smelling thyme, watching the ferry Omeros round the cape widdershins, always wanting names for at least the least movable aspects of this. When "this" is especially complicated I still want the name, sometimes enough to make it up. That is a poem, not the only kind, but a kind that begins from a place whose name experience suddenly reveals as inadequate, like "Tintern Abbey," "Penshurst," *Paterson*, "Cape Breton," "London," "America." Well—that is a way to make oneself at home, or make a home for oneself. It is also useful not to forget the feet. Home, if we make a place home by learning every step of it, is unconscious geography.

Notes

"Tambourine" was composed between February 19 and May 30, 1999, with final editing on June 20. It participates in the tradition of "pi mnemonics": The length of each successive word is determined by the decimal digits of pi (3.14...; therefore, "Now I walk..."). A zero dictates the end of a sentence/stanza; multiple zeroes dictate section divisions and are indicated within the section dividing line. Punctuation is excluded; line-breaks are free, but each one entails an additional indent from the left margin. The title is taken from Patrick Leigh Fermor, *Roumeli: Travels in Northern Greece* (1966, rpt. Penguin 1983), p. 230:

> The Dodecanese is a sea-song by twelve sponge-fishers; Antikythera a mermaid forsaken; Skopelos, a lobster's and Poros, a mock-turtle's song; Aegina a tambourine.

The "Eight Greek Lyrics" were written during a first, four-month visit to Greece in the fall of 1997, on the stylistic model of Yannis Ritsos's *Parodos* —which in a different way inspired "Morning Noon & Night." (See "On Becoming a Greek Poet," *Southwest Review*, Winter 1998.) The faults in the Greek are as few as they are only thanks to the patience of Dimitra Dimitra, Iphiyenia Tournavitos, Peter Mackridge, and George and Sofia Simatos. The proverbs in two of the poems are quoted from *Moon Over Morocco*, by ZBS Media (1975).

My thanks to Menelaos and Hildegard Xinotroulias for their hospitality during the composition of this book.

Acknowledgments

Poems from this book have appeared previously in *Field, New American Writing, Pleiades,* and *Yale Review,* and online at the *New American Writing* and *Jacket* websites. "Where Am I" originally appeared in *Southwest Review.*

About the Author

Charles O. Hartman has published five previous books of poems (including one collaboration with Hugh Kenner "with computer interventions"). His books of prose include *Free Verse: An Essay on Prosody; Jazz Text: Voice and Improvisation in Poetry, Jazz, and Song;* and *Virtual Muse: Experiments in Computer Poetry.* Professor of English and Poet in Residence at Connecticut College, he plays jazz guitar when time allows and gigs arise.

Ahsahta Press

SAWTOOTH POETRY PRIZE SERIES

2002: AARON MCCOLLOUGH, *Welkin* (Brenda Hillman, judge)
2003: GRAHAM FOUST, *Leave the Room to Itself* (Joe Wenderoth, judge)

NEW SERIES

DAN BEACHY-QUICK, *Spell*
LISA FISHMAN, *Dear, Read*
PEGGY HAMILTON, *Forbidden City*
CHARLES O. HARTMAN, *Island*
LANCE PHILLIPS, *Corpus Socius*
HEATHER SELLERS, *Drinking Girls and Their Dresses*
LIZ WALDNER, *Saving the Appearances*

MODERN AND CONTEMPORARY POETRY OF THE AMERICAN WEST

SANDRA ALCOSSER, *A Fish to Feed All Hunger*
DAVID AXELROD, *Jerusalem of Grass*
DAVID BAKER, *Laws of the Land*
DICK BARNES, *Few and Far Between*
CONGER BEASLEY, JR., *Over DeSoto's Bones*
LINDA BIERDS, *Flights of the Harvest-Mare*
RICHARD BLESSING, *Winter Constellations*
BOYER, BURMASTER, AND TRUSKY, EDS., *The Ahsahta Anthology*
PEGGY POND CHURCH, *New and Selected Poems*
KATHARINE COLES, *The One Right Touch*
WYN COOPER, *The Country of Here Below*
CRAIG COTTER, *Chopstix Numbers*

Judson Crews, *The Clock of Moss*

H.L. Davis, *Selected Poems*

Susan Strayer Deal, *The Dark is a Door*

Susan Strayer Deal, *No Moving Parts*

Linda Dyer, *Fictional Teeth*

Gretel Ehrlich, *To Touch the Water*

Gary Esarey, *How Crows Talk and Willows Walk*

Julie Fay, *Portraits of Women*

Thomas Hornsby Ferril, *Anvil of Roses*

Thomas Hornsby Ferril, *Westering*

Hildegarde Flanner, *The Hearkening Eye*

Charley John Greasybear, *Songs*

Corrinne Hales, *Underground*

Hazel Hall, *Selected Poems*

Nan Hannon, *Sky River*

Gwendolen Haste, *Selected Poems*

Kevin Hearle, *Each Thing We Know Is Changed Because We
    Know It And Other Poems*

Sonya Hess, *Kingdom of Lost Waters*

Cynthia Hogue, *The Woman in Red*

Robert Krieger, *Headlands, Rising*

Elio Emiliano Ligi, *Disturbances*

Haniel Long, *My Seasons*

Ken McCullough, *Sycamore•Oriole*

Norman McLeod, *Selected Poems*

Barbara Meyn, *The Abalone Heart*

David Mutschlecner, *Esse*

Dixie Partridge, *Deer in the Haystacks*

Gerrye Payne, *The Year-God*

George Perreault, *Curved Like an Eye*

Howard W. Robertson, *to the fierce guard in the Assyrian Saloon*

Leo Romero, *Agua Negra*

Leo Romero, *Going Home Away Indian*

Miriam Sagan, *The Widow's Coat*

Philip St. Clair, *At the Tent of Heaven*

Philip St. Clair, *Little-Dog-of-Iron*

Donald Schenker, *Up Here*

Gary Short, *Theory of Twilight*

D.J. Smith, *Prayers for the Dead Ventriloquist*

Richard Speakes, *Hannah's Travel*

Genevieve Taggard, *To the Natural World*

Tom Trusky, ed., *Women Poets of the West*

Marnie Walsh, *A Taste of the Knife*

Bill Witherup, *Men at Work*

Carolyne Wright, *Stealing the Children*

This book is set in Apollo and Minion Pro Greek type
with Bauer Bodoni titles
by Ahsahta Press at Boise State University
and manufactured on acid-free paper
by Boise State University Printing and Graphics, Boise, Idaho.

AHSAHTA PRESS

2004

JANET HOLMES, DIRECTOR

SCOTT ABELS

JOHN OTTEY

J. REUBEN APPELMAN

ERICH SCHWEIKHER

SANDY FRIEDLY

AMY WEGNER

WENDY GREEN

MARY HICKMAN, INTERN

MARIE MOYER

AMY GARRETT, INTERN

BRANDON NOLTA

MIA WRIGHT, INTERN